ACTS: The Body in Action

ACTS: The Body in Action

A Discussion Guide
for
Home Bible Study

By
David Burnham
and
Sue Burnham

MOODY PRESS
CHICAGO

Printed in the United States of America

Contents

INTRODUCTION

This discussion guide is designed to lead group Bible studies into a clear understanding of each passage in the book of Acts. Also, it provides opportunity for each student to apply the biblical teachings to his personal life.

SUGGESTIONS FOR GROUP BIBLE STUDY

1. Designate one person to be discussion leader. Rotate discussion leaders weekly. Each different personality will make its own unique contribution to the discussion.
2. The discussion leader asks the questions suggested in this guide. After members of the group have made their contributions, the leader can proceed to the next question.
3. Read each section of the Bible aloud before discussing the question. The discussion leader can ask for volunteers to read.
4. You may refer to various translations of the Bible, but do not consult other studies or commentaries during the discussion.
5. Stick to the passage under discussion. As the study progresses, you may refer back to preceding portions of the book of Acts.
6. Stay on target and avoid tangents. Sharing is important, but long discussions of other subjects can lead away from the main emphasis in a passage.
7. Encourage each member to take part in the discussion. Each member must be concerned and disciplined to listen and participate.
8. Begin and end the study at the agreed time. Allow enough time for the main points in each section and the conclusion.

LESSON 1

INTRODUCING THE BOOK OF ACTS

The book of Acts was written by Luke around A.D. 62-64. The Acts describes the continuation of the ministry of the risen Christ Jesus through His Spirit-filled followers. This book bridges the gap between the gospels and the epistles, and in vivid, rapid description, the growth of the early church is accurately recorded.

1. Describe Luke from the three references about him in the New Testament:

   Colossians 4:14—"Luke, the beloved physician, and Demas, greet you."

   _____

   2 Timothy 4:11—"Only Luke is with me."

   _____

   Philemon 24—"Marcus, Aristarchus, Demas, Lucas, my fellowlabourers."

   _____

2. Are there any admirable characteristics of Luke indicated in these verses?

   _____

READ Luke 1:1-4

3. Luke's first volume of the history of Christian origins is the gospel of Luke. To whom did Luke write the first volume?

_____

4. Describe Theophilus._____

5. What credentials did Luke have for writing this historical volume?

_____

6. In verse 4, what did Luke state as his purpose in writing? Does it give you confidence to know the truth about your belief?

_____

READ Acts 1:1-2

7. What was included in Luke's first volume to Theophilus? Name some of the things Jesus did and taught. How did Luke conclude the first treatise?

_____

_____

8. Luke wrote the second volume of the history of Christian origins, entitled Acts. To whom did he write the second treatise?

_____

READ Acts 1:8

9. After the resurrection of Jesus, Luke carried the progress report of Christianity through a period of thirty years. What was the apostolic commission that was followed and recorded for the thirty year duration?

_____

10. How inclusive was the commission?

_____

APPLICATION

Are there any certainties in your faith?

_____

PREPARATION FOR THE CHURCH

The first chapter of Acts includes the final instructions to the apostles during the forty days following the resurrection. The chapter also describes Christ's ascension and the apostles waiting for the coming of the Holy Spirit, who would empower them for service.

READ 1:1-3

1. What did Jesus do during the forty days following His resurrection? What proof did Jesus offer of His bodily resurrection (see Luke 24:36-45)?

_____

READ 1:4-8

2. What command did Jesus give to the apostles? Is waiting ever important in your life? What promise did Jesus give?

_____

3. As a result of the kingdom discussions, what question was raised by the apostles? Why didn't Jesus give them a specific time limit? Should Christians today seek to know the future?

_____

_____

4. What did Jesus emphasize as the new task for the disciples to perform? What power would enable them to perform mighty works and preach effectively?

_____

READ 1:9-14

5. Describe the ascension of Jesus. Was it a sudden vanishing? Read Exodus 40:34 for an explanation of the cloud.

_____

6. Who comforted the apostles? What hope was offered?

_____

7. Where did the ascension take place? Who was in the upper room waiting for the Holy Spirit? What was the chief activity during this time? What characterized their prayer meeting? What do you do when you are anxious?

_____

_____

READ 1:15-22

8. Who was the spokesman for the 120 followers of Jesus staying in the upper room? Why was there a vacancy among the apostles?

_____

9. To what did Peter refer as his authority for finding a replacement for Judas? What were the essential qualifications of the successor?

_____

READ 1:23-26

10. Who fit the requirements? Why did the disciples pray? For what purpose do you pray? Did the apostles pass judgment on the destiny of Judas?

_____

11. After prayer, what procedure common to that day did the apostles use to choose Matthias? Was the choosing of the twelfth apostle done haphazardly?

_____

SUMMARY

What were the instructions Jesus gave before He ascended to heaven?

_____

What hope did Jesus leave His followers?

_____

APPLICATION

This week pray before making little and big decisions. Take note of the outcome.

PENTECOST

Pentecost (which comes from the word meaning "fiftieth") was the feast occurring fifty days after the Passover Sabbath. It commemorated the harvest. On Pentecost the disciples were waiting for the Holy Spirit, as instructed by Jesus, when the promise was fulfilled. On this day they were empowered for the task to "be witnesses" (Acts 1:8).

READ 2:1-13

1. Describe the believers on the day of Pentecost. What unique event took place? What were the audible and visible signs of the arrival of the Holy Spirit?

   _____

2. What was the outward evidence of the disciples' being filled with the Holy Ghost?

   _____

3. Who was at Jerusalem for a feast? How did the Holy Spirit use the tongues of the believers?

   _____

4. Why were the hearers seized with amazement? How many different nationalities were represented? What effect would this event have in the spread of Christianity? What message were the believers uttering as they spoke in other tongues?

_____

_____

5. How did some of the hearers explain the strange behavior of the believers? How do some people today react to the evidence of the power of God?

_____

READ 2:14-21

6. How did Peter reason with the multitude that the believers were not drunk? How did he explain the miraculous event in a way that the Jews would understand? What signs will yet occur? When?

_____

_____

READ 2:22-36

7. What works of Jesus did Peter mention as proof that Jesus was the Messiah (v. 22)?

_____

8. What hope was foretold by David concerning Christ (v. 31)?

_____

9. How was the Lordship of Christ Jesus demonstrated on the Day of Pentecost (v. 36)?

_____

READ 2:37-41

10. What happened to the hearers after the message of Peter had been delivered? What instruction did Peter give to the inquirers?

_____

11. An essential factor in conversion is repentance (Acts 3:19). What does it mean to repent? What was the outward symbol that conversion had occurred? What gift did every convert receive? How many responded?

_____

_____

READ 2:42-47

12. What was the general activity of the believers? What principle of sharing evolved? What were the believers' attitudes?

_____

13. What relationship did the believers have with all people? Do you think there was snobbishness?

_____

14. How often did the new church take in new members? Who could join?

_____

SUMMARY

What promise was fulfilled on the day of Pentecost as a sign to the Jews?

_____

What do you conclude about Jesus from the proofs that Peter presented?

_____

In what ways does your life-style differ from that of the early believers?

_____

APPLICATION

Put into practice one activity of the early church, and keep a record of the outcome.

THE FIRST CHURCH MIRACLE

Luke gives a fuller account of one of the wonders (Acts 2:43) done through the apostles which received considerable publicity. This miracle was performed as an opportunity to "be witnesses" (Acts 1:8).

READ 3:1-10

1. Where and when did the first apostolic miracle take place? Who did Peter and John see at the Beautiful Gate? What was his condition? What have you observed on your way into your church?

   _____

2. How did the lame man get the attention of the apostles? What did Peter command (v. 4)? What valuable gift did Peter desire to give? What do you value that money cannot buy?

   _____

   _____

3. Describe the steps of healing the lame man. What was the response of the Temple crowd?

   _____

READ 3:11-16

4. Where did Peter preach his second sermon? Was the miracle due to the apostles' superior godliness? How did Peter appeal to the Jews in his sermon?

_____

_____

5. What approach did Peter use in challenging the crowd? How did Peter contrast men's treatment of Christ and God's treatment of Him? Is there a contrast today?

_____

_____

6. What did the lame man have to do in order to benefit from the power of Jesus Christ working through the apostles?

_____

READ 3:17-26

7. What excuse does Peter give the crowd? Did Peter and John identify themselves with the Jewish rulers?

_____

8. Of what fulfillment did Peter remind them (cf. Isaiah 53)?

_____

9. How could the hearers be pardoned from their part in the death of Christ? What did Peter say was the result of repentance?

_____

10. What prophets foretold the miracle of Christ?

_____

11. What did Peter characterize as the special qualities of the Jews? Were the Jews favored?

_____

12. What requirement did God fulfill through Jesus for bringing blessing to the Jews? How can you find blessing from God?

_____

SUMMARY

Why do you think this miracle was performed?

_____

Note the names of Jesus in this sermon (vv. 14, 15, 18, 22). Which one is most meaningful to you?

_____

APPLICATION

Can you walk or leap or read or hear? This week praise God for blessings and keep a record of them.

THE FIRST PERSECUTION

The captain of the Temple was responsible for maintaining order, like a chief of police, in the Temple courts. The Sadducees were the aristocrats of the Jewish supreme court called the Sanhedrin. The arrest of Peter and John by these authorities was a result of being witnesses (Acts 1:8).

READ 4:1-12

1. What happened to the apostles as Peter was preaching? Was there a reason for the arrest? Who was particularly disturbed (cf. Mark 12:18)?

2. What were the results of the healing and sermon to the hearers and to the apostles? What outcome have you received from hardship?

3. What three groups made up the Sanhedrin (official ruling body of the Jewish nation)? Who was the high priest? Read John 18:13-24 for Annas's trial of Jesus a few weeks earlier.

4. What question was put to the apostles? How did fearful Peter become bold?

_____

5. What facts did Peter's testimony present? Why was Peter's reference to Christ, the Living Stone, appropriate for reasoning with the Sanhedrin?

_____

_____

6. Would God offer another provision for salvation? What is God's provision for salvation?

_____

READ 4:13-18

7. What evidence revealed an association of the apostles with Jesus? Why was this situation a disturbing one for the Sanhedrin?

_____

8. What warning was given the apostles? How would you feel if you had been warned not to speak of Christ?

_____

READ 4:19-22

9. Describe the response of Peter and John (cf. Jeremiah 20:9). Did Peter and John receive praise?

_____

READ 4:23-31

10. How did the apostles address God in their prayer of praise? What recognition did they give Jesus?

_____

11. Did the apostles ask God for an escape from the Sanhedrin's threats? How was their request answered? (This was not a new baptism.)

_____

READ 4:32-37

12. Was communism legislated? What brought the union of hearts (see John 17:21)?

_____

13. What was the apostles' emphasis as they witnessed? Is the resurrection important to you?

_____

14. How was a generous spirit revealed among the believers?

_____

SUMMARY

What were the essentials in the testimony of the apostles before the Sanhedrin?

_____

What characterized the Christians' prayer?

_____

APPLICATION

Ask God for boldness to speak for Jesus and note the results.

DISCIPLINE IN THE CHURCH

The Holy Spirit manifested His power with a demand for holiness in the lives of the believers. The incidents in this chapter reveal the work of the Holy Spirit as the believers continued to follow the command to "be witnesses" (Acts 1:8).

READ 5:1-11

1. Describe the plot of Ananias and Sapphira. Who detected the lie? Were they under obligation to sell their property?

   _____

2. Did they have the right to retain part of the price for their private use? To whom did they lie?

   _____

3. What do you think Ananias and Sapphira hoped to gain by this act (Acts 4:36-37)?

   _____

4. Who brought judgment? How did this event reveal God's attitude toward sin? What effect did this have upon the church? Does God discipline the believer today (see 1 Corinthians 11:30-32)?

_____

_____

READ 5:12-16

5. Where did the believers have their public gatherings? How did God bless them?

_____

6. Can the church expect blessing from God today?

_____

READ 5:17-28

7. From what did the second persecution proceed? Describe the intervention of the angel.

_____

8, On what two charges did the high priest question the apostles?

_____

READ 5:29-33

9. Upon what facts did Peter's defense rest? Contrast the description of Jesus by the high priest (v. 28) and the description Peter stated. Has there been an occasion in your life when you obeyed God rather than man?

_____

READ 5:34-39

10. How was the anger of the Sanhedrin softened? Describe the credentials of Gamaliel.

_____

11. What policy did Gamaliel propose? Do you agree with Gamaliel's formula?

_____

READ 5:40-42

12. How did the apostles react to the beatings? How did they continue to fulfill the commission of Acts 1:8?

_____

SUMMARY

What additional facts can be learned about the Holy Spirit from the incident of Ananias and Sapphira?

_____

What facts can be learned about Jesus from the apostles' description in verses 30-31?

_____

APPLICATION

Examine yourself for spiritual dishonesty. "If a man therefore purge himself from these, he shall be a vessel unto honour, sanctified, and meet for the master's use, and prepared unto every good work" (2 Timothy 2:21).

SELECTION FOR SERVICE

Stephen was chosen as one of the seven to perform a special task. His teaching drove a wedge between Judaism and Christianity which brought distinctiveness to the Christian church. The work of the seven freed the apostles for their primary task to "be witnesses" (Acts 1:8).

READ 6:1-7

1. What complaint arose within the Christian community?

   _____

2. Describe the procedure the apostles used to eliminate the rift. Why did the apostles give the administration responsibilities to others?

   _____

3. How many men were to assume this responsibility? What were their qualifications?

   _____

4. What were the important tasks of the twelve apostles? What tasks do you think religious leaders should perform today?

   _____

5. What form did the apostles use to discharge the seven for their special duty (cf. Numbers 27:23)? Name the various ways that God can be served.

_____

6. What progress was made in the Christian community? From which group did many new believers in Christ come? How could this be a problem?

_____

READ 6:8-15

7. What was Stephen's reputation? Which people began a dispute with him? What was the outcome of the debate?

_____

8. What course did Stephen's opponents adopt? What were the first accusations?

_____

9. What claims were brought against him in the council? (The charges, which were subtle misrepresentations of the words actually spoken, will be clarified in Acts 7.)

_____

10. Describe the face of Stephen. Who saw it?

_____

31

SUMMARY

Review the work of the apostles and the appointed seven.

_____

_____

Describe Stephen from verses 5, 8, 10, and 15. What characteristics did he have that you admire?

_____

_____

APPLICATION

Count the opportunities you have to serve God daily. Keep a
record of the opportunities you use.

THE FIRST MARTYR

Stephen's defense before the Sanhedrin was a historical review of the Jewish nation from the call of Abraham to the building of Solomon's Temple. The Jewish history revealed the plan of God and its fulfillment in Jesus. Stephen's defense was an opportunity to be a witness (Acts 1:8).

READ 7:1-16

1. How did Stephen refute the charge of blasphemy against God in this section? What were God's promises that Abraham believed (vv. 5, 8)?

_____

_____

2. How did God continue His purpose in spite of the patriarchs' envious hearts toward Joseph? Where were the patriarchs buried? Can you believe the Words of God, as Abraham did, without a tangible object in which to trust?

_____

READ 7:17-29

3. What circumstances in Egypt brought discomfort to the Israelites? Describe God's appointed deliverer.

_____

4. Did the Israelites accept Moses as their deliverer? How did Stephen portray similar situations of Moses (v. 25) and Joseph (v. 9)? How had the Jews repeated the same pattern toward Christ (Acts 2:22-24)?

_____

_____

READ 7:30-43

5. Describe Moses' encounter with God. What message did he receive?

_____

6. What evidence was revealed to the Israelites and Egyptians as proof of Moses' authority from God?

_____

7. Examine Stephen's quotation from the Old Testament in verse 37. Who believed Moses' words? Who had been unwilling to keep the Law? How did this counteract the Sanhedrin's accusations in Acts 6:11, 13?

_____

_____

8. What was God's response to the Israelites' choice to worship idols made by their hands? Are there people today who choose to worship idols? What are the consequences?

_____

_____

READ 7:44-53

9. How did Stephen criticize the Jews' most cherished glory? Where did God deal with His people before the Temple existed (Acts 7:2, 9, 30, 36)? How do people today restrict God?

_____

_____

10. How did Stephen apply his message to the Jewish nation? Of what deeds did he accuse them which were worse than those of their fathers?

_____

READ 7:54-60

11. How was the truth of the resurrection proclaimed by Stephen's vision? What mob violence occurred?

_____

12. For what two matters did Stephen pray? How did this prayer follow the example of Jesus (see Luke 23:34, 46)? Can you imagine what you might have prayed in Stephen's circumstances?

_____

SUMMARY

How did Stephen's defense prove that the presence of God is not restricted to any one land or any material building?

_____

Compare the attitude of the Jewish people toward God's messengers in the Old Testament, and their attitude toward Jesus as Messiah.

_____

_____

APPLICATION

Are there any idols in your life such as a piece of wood, a picture, a book, a piece of furniture, or a building? Confess your idol, forsake it, and ask God to give you faith in the Word of God.

PHILIP, THE EVANGELIST

Following Stephen's death, the Pharisees joined the Sadducees in a campaign to repress the church at Jerusalem. The persecution brought about the beginning of fulfilling Christ's commission "to be witnesses unto me both in Jerusalem and in all Judea, and in Samaria, and unto the uttermost part of the earth" (Acts 1:8).

READ 8:1-3

1. How did Stephen's death move the church toward her task of evangelism?

_____

2. Who was one of the chief leaders of the persecution? Describe his persistency.

_____

READ 8:4-8

3. What was the main activity of the dispersed Christians?

_____

4. How did Philip reveal boldness (see John 4:9)? What was accomplished in Samaria? How can unfriendly relations be reconciled today?

_____

_____

READ 8:9-13

5. What was the reputation of Simon? What actions of Philip impressed Simon? Contrast the motives of Philip (v. 5) and Simon (vv. 9-11). Is it possible today for individuals who profess to be religious leaders to desire power in order to exalt self rather than Christ?

_____

_____

READ 8:14-25

6. Who was sent to inspect the work at Samaria? Did the Samaritans exercise saving faith before the apostles came from Jerusalem (vv. 12, 14)?

_____

7. What confirmation did the Samaritan Christians receive which brought assurance of incorporation into the new community of the people of God?

_____

38

8. What power did Simon desire? Explain the reason for Simon's limitation in understanding the truth. What rebuke and alternative did Peter offer? What was Simon's concern?

_____

_____

READ 8:26-40

9. Where did Philip go under divine guidance? Describe the eunuch. What was his request?

_____

10. How did Philip explain the Old Testament prophecy of Isaiah 53:7-8?

_____

11. What verbal confession did the eunuch state? What was his public identification with Christ? Why do you think the Holy Spirit led Philip to this eunuch?

_____

_____

12. Where was the eunuch looking for answers? Do you believe God will show you answers when you search the Scriptures?

_____

SUMMARY

In this chapter, what progress was made in fulfilling the Great Commission (vv. 4, 5, 25, 27, 40)?

_____

List the verbs in Acts 8:27, 30 which describe Philip's obedience to the Holy Spirit.

_____

APPLICATION

Study the example of Philip with the eunuch to learn the principles of evangelism. Pray for an opportunity to serve Christ in this manner.

CONVERSION OF PAUL

Saul was born a Hebrew. He had as good an education as Judaism offered. He knew Hellenistic culture and was a Roman citizen. Saul, in due time, gave all that he was to Christ and followed the command to "be witnesses" (Acts 1:8).

READ 9:1-9

1. Where did Saul's fury against the Christians lead him? What commission did he desire from the high priest?

   _____

2. How did Luke describe Christianity (v. 2)? What does that term mean to you?

   _____

3. What did Saul see and hear outside the city of Damascus? How personal was the voice?

   _____

4. What evidence proved the reality of Saul's experience?

   _____

READ 9:10-19a

5. Describe the visions that the Lord gave Ananias and Saul. Did Ananias have a valid reason to protest?

_____

_____

6. For what great work did the Lord choose Saul? Why would Saul have to suffer? Would you be willing to be a Saul?

_____

7. Describe the uniqueness of Saul's commissioning by Ananias to serve the Lord. Why do you think Saul was blinded?

_____

READ 9:19b-22

8. What did Saul openly proclaim about Jesus? Compare the outcome of Saul's trip to Damascus with his original intention (Acts 9:1-2).

_____

_____

READ 9:23-25

9. What adventure is experienced by Saul? Why would the Jews of Damascus be exceptionally angry?

_____

READ 9:26-31

10. What dilemma did Saul face with the disciples and with his old friends in Jerusalem? How was Barnabas true to his name (cf. Acts 4:36-37)? How did Saul's new friends help him?

_____

_____

11. Name the characteristics of the church. Are these qualities in evidence today?

_____

READ 9:32-43

12. What miracles resulted in belief in Jesus Christ for the people of Lydda, Sharon, and Joppa? How had Dorcas endeared herself to the people of Joppa?

_____

SUMMARY

Summarize the change in Saul (Acts 9:1, 22).

_____

How did the believers help each other (Acts 9:17, 25, 27, 34, 36, 38, 40)?

_____

APPLICATION

Be aware of opportunities to serve other believers. Keep a record of opportunities used.

THE CONVERSION OF CORNELIUS

The apostolic message reached the Gentiles, beginning with Cornelius in the city of Caesarea. The Jewish-Gentile barrier was crossed as Peter continued to be a witness (Acts 1:8).

READ 10:1-8

1. What kind of position did Cornelius hold? Name his virtues.

_____

2. Who came to Cornelius in a vision? What was the message from God? Was Cornelius's devotion to God rewarded? How did Cornelius respond?

_____

_____

READ 10:9-16

3. What traditional food-laws did Peter follow (cf. Leviticus 11)? Describe Peter's vision as to what beasts were in the sheet, and what Peter was to do with the beasts. Were the beasts clean or unclean? In summary, what did God teach Peter about ceremonialism?

_____

_____

READ 10:17-23a

4. How did the Holy Spirit interpret the vision when Peter was perplexed? What assurance did the Holy Spirit provide concerning Peter's association with Gentiles?

_____

_____

5. How did Peter step across the barrier of Jewish prejudice in obedience? What can God do for your prejudice?

_____

READ 10:23b-33

6. How many witnesses did Peter take with him (Acts 11:12)? Did Cornelius have witnesses? How did Peter disclaim any worship of himself?

_____

_____

7. When Peter violated Jewish tradition, what confidence did he have? Where is your confidence in facing new situations?

_____

8. Describe the ideal church from verse 33.

_____

READ 10:34-43

9. How was Peter's message especially directed toward the Gentiles (vv. 34-36, 43)? Describe the message by Peter.

_____

10. How could the Gentiles receive remission of their sins? Would the virtues of Cornelius (v. 2) provide him with salvation?

_____

READ 10:44-48

11. What confirmation was given to the Gentiles that salvation could be theirs through belief in Jesus Christ?

_____

12. Who were surprised that the Gentiles could be recipients of the Holy Spirit?

_____

13. What was the outward expression of belief in Christ?

_____

SUMMARY

How did the nullifying of the laws of cleanness prepare Peter to reach the Gentiles?

_____

Why do you think God chose Cornelius to fulfill His commission to the Gentiles?

_____

APPLICATION

Are you willing to ask God for help in overcoming your prejudice? Keep a record of His direction and your obedience.

CHRISTIANS IN ANTIOCH

The gospel continued its outreach into Phenice and Cyprus and Antioch as believers obeyed the commission to "be witnesses."

READ 11:1-18

1. What was the reaction of the Jews in Jerusalem toward the salvation of the Gentiles in Caesarea? What was the main point of contention?

   _____

2. Why do you think Luke repeated the account of Peter's encounter with the Gentiles? How did the memory of God's Word confirm the validity of the Gentiles' experience (v. 16)?

   _____

3. Whose will was accomplished? What replaced criticism in the hearts of the listeners?

   _____

READ 11:19-26

4. Describe the far-reaching results of Stephen's death. How can God take the circumstance of death and use it to His glory today?

_____

5. Who was sent to Antioch? How did he qualify for this special assignment?

_____

6. What did he observe? What advice did he offer?

_____

7. Who did Barnabas choose as a colleague? What work did Barnabas and Saul accomplish?

_____

8. What reputation was established by the believers in Antioch? What type of a program do you think would be necessary to establish a believer in the faith in one year?

_____

READ 11:27-30

9. What prophecy did Agabus, under the direction of the Holy Spirit, give? How did the Christians at Antioch express faith in the prophecy?

_____

10. Who participated in aiding the Judaean brethren? How was Barnabas a good choice for leader in this situation (cf. Acts 4:36)? What help does God give in difficult times?

_____

_____

SUMMARY

What does the term "repentance unto life" (v. 18) mean to you?

_____

What does the word "Christian" mean?

_____

Describe the leadership of Barnabas in verses 23-26, 30; see also Acts 4:36; 9:27.

_____

_____

APPLICATION

Could the foundation of Barnabas's usefulness to God have rested upon his unselfish heart? Check your life for selfishness, and ask God for release from self in order to serve Him. Record the results.

THE HERODIAN PERSECUTION

The Sadducees and Pharisees were influential Jewish parties who persecuted the believers. The third group who attacked the Christians were the Herodians, led by Herod Agrippa I. To find favor with the Jews, Herod Agrippa I made a pretense of observing the Law. The persecutions continued to move the believers to "be witnesses" (Acts 1:8).

READ 12:1-19

1. How did Herod Agrippa I show anger toward the church? What indicates the charge against James was civil and not religious? In what way could the charge have been disloyalty to the government (see Acts 5:29)?

   _____

   _____

2. How did Herod Agrippa I please the Jews? Why did the authorities take extra precautions in guarding Peter (cf. Acts 5:18-20)? Why did Herod postpone killing Peter?

   _____

   _____

3. Contrast the weapons used by Herod against the church and those used by the church in defense. Give a description of the prayer offered by the believers in verse 5.

_____

_____

4. How could an angel be identified (see also Acts 10:30)? Examine the account carefully and name the miracles recorded in verses 6-10.

_____

_____

5. From whom was Peter delivered? Why do you think he went to the house of Mary? Where do you go when you are freed from a difficulty?

_____

6. How did the believers react to answered prayer? Can God answer prayer today even when you are doubting?

_____

7. How was Herod's image among the Jews altered?

_____

READ 12:20-25

8. Why did Tyre and Sidon need to make public peace with Herod?

_____

53

9. Did Herod repudiate the flattery of the crowd when they called him 'god'? (Herod had posed as a nominal Jew, and his acceptance of worship was blasphemy.) What was the judgment of God?

_____

10. Contrast the miserable end of Herod and the advancement of the Word of God. Can the enemy prevail against God?

_____

11. Who fulfilled their task in conclusion of the account in Acts 11:30?

_____

SUMMARY

Describe the two persecutions (vv. 2, 4). Which persecution was the most severe for a Christian?

_____

Evaluate the character of Herod Agrippa I shown in Acts 12:1-4, 19-21.

_____

APPLICATION

For a specific period of time, pray without ceasing to God for an individual and record the results.

FIRST MISSIONARY JOURNEY

Two of the most gifted men of the church were selected as missionaries. Saul (referred to as Paul by the Gentiles) and Barnabas were fulfilling Christ's commission to "be witnesses ... unto the uttermost part of the earth" (Acts 1:8).

READ 13:1-3

1. What direction did the Holy Spirit give concerning the work of Barnabas and Saul? When did the Holy Spirit communicate His will?

   _____

2. How was fellowship expressed as Paul and Barnabas were released for new work?

   _____

READ 13:4-12

3. To whose home territory did they sail (Acts 4:36)? Contrast the purpose in heart of Elymas and Sergius Paulus.

   _____

4. Describe the verbal rebuke that Paul gave Elymas. How was blindness a symbol of his spiritual condition? What benefits come from blindness?

_____

5. Was Elymas ignorant of God? Who responded to spiritual light?

_____

READ 13:13-23

6. Who assisted Paul and Barnabas, but returned to Jerusalem from Perga? Where did the missionaries go when they entered into a new city (Acts 13:5, 13)?

_____

7. What history did Paul emphasize concerning the promise of Jesus the Messiah? Name the acts of God which revealed His love for Israel.

_____

_____

READ 13:24-37

8. What was the testimony of John the Baptist concerning Jesus? What rejection was a fulfillment of prophecy?

_____

9. What were the glad tidings Paul expressed to the people? What proof did he present of the resurrection of Jesus? What comparison did Paul make between the beloved King David and Jesus?

_____

_____

READ 13:38-41

10. After reminding the people of Jewish history and fulfilled prophecy, how did Paul apply this new message to them personally? What new elements are described in Paul's message of application? Describe how you imagine the Jewish people felt hearing that Christ could release them from the Law of Moses.

_____

_____

READ 13:42-52

11. What was the result of the missionaries' message to the Gentiles and to the Jews? How did the Jewish leaders react? How did Paul put into practice his teaching in Romans 1:16?

_____

_____

12. What attitude did the missionaries have toward persecution? How did God encourage the disciples?

_____

SUMMARY

Summarize the difficulties encountered by the missionaries on their first trip (vv. 8, 13, 45, 50).

_____

_____

Name the positive results from their efforts for God (vv. 12, 44, 48, 52).

_____

APPLICATION

This week keep a record of God's encouragement through difficulties in serving Christ.

MISSIONARY WORK IN ICONIUM, LYSTRA, AND DERBE

Barnabas and Paul penetrated more definitely into Gentile territory. They endured the results of divisions among the people as they preached Christ and performed wonders in His Name as they continued to "be witnesses" (Acts 1:8).

READ 14:1-5

1. What familiar pattern did Barnabas and Paul follow in Iconium (Acts 13:14)? Who was in the congregation?

   _____

2. Who responded to the message? By what means did the unbelieving Jews stir up the Gentiles? What action was contemplated?

   _____

   _____

3. What indicated divine approval of the work of the missionaries? Do you know when you are pleasing Christ?

   _____

READ 14:6-20a

4. Where did they continue to preach the gospel? What specific miracle was performed by Paul, as generalized in verse 3? What preceded this miracle? (Read Acts 3 and note the difference in the order of events.)

_____

_____

5. What effect did this miracle have upon the observers? Because of superstition, who did the people of Lystra believe Barnabas and Paul were? Why were Barnabas and Paul unaware of the preparation for sacrifice?

_____

_____

6. How were Paul's actions and address fitting to the peasants? Compare this sermon in content and length to the sermon at Antioch in Acts 13.

_____

7. Did Paul's sermon dissuade the people from offering sacrifices? Who pursued Barnabas and Paul and instigated a stoning? How were the peasants led into contradictory actions? What influences are at work in your life? To which do you respond?

_____

_____

8. Describe Paul's recovery from stoning.

_____

READ 20b-21a

9. What did the missionaries experience in Derbe?

_____

READ 21b-28

10. Why did the missionaries retrace their steps into danger-
    ous territory? What warnings did Paul give the converts?

_____

11. How were the churches organized? How do you think an
    elapse of time prepared new converts for church ap-
    pointments?

_____

12. What type of reception did the missionaries have back at
    Antioch? What did they emphasize in their report? If not
    through circumcision, how were the Gentiles to be ad-
    mitted to the church?

_____

_____

SUMMARY

What divisions among the people caused Barnabas and Paul much tribulation (vv. 2, 4, 5, 19)?

_____

Review the variety of work of the missionaries (vv. 1, 3, 22-23, 27).

_____

APPLICATION

Do you have a friend who needs to be strengthened in the faith? Write a letter, call on the telephone, or visit your friend this week. Pray for him and keep a record of the results.

THE COUNCIL AT JERUSALEM AND THE PHILIPPIAN CHURCH

Paul, the statesman, helped set up a center for problem solving in Jerusalem and applied the decisions of the council in an orderly fashion. Godly decision making and right responses to difficulties were ways the evangelistic team obeyed the commission to "be witnesses" (Acts 1:8).

READ 15:1-5

1. What plan did some men design for salvation? How did Paul and Barnabas respond? How is the concern of the church of Antioch reflected?

_____

_____

2. How was the news of salvation of the Gentiles received by the various churches? What was the opinion of the Pharisees concerning Gentile converts?

_____

READ 15:6-18

3. What basics did Peter emphasize in declaring God's plan of salvation? How did James validate his statements?

_____

63

READ 15:19-35

4. What four requirements did James place upon the Gentiles so as not to offend the Jews and bring about unity? How was the message communicated to the church of Antioch?

_____

_____

5. What reaction did the message bring? How would the council's decision affect the opinionated teachers from Judea?

_____

6. What can be learned about church problem-solving by the example of Antioch? In what similar situations today must a Christian be willing to abstain for the sake of not offending?

_____

READ 15:36-41

7. How would a return to the established churches be profitable following the Jerusalem Council?

_____

8. What good did God work out of the disagreement of Paul and Barnabas? (Read 1 Corinthians 9:6 and Colossians 4:10 to note later reconciliation.) How would Silas be an asset to Paul (see Acts 15:27 and 16:37)? What was the benefit of the visit?

_____

_____

READ 16:1-5

9. Describe the background and reputation of Timothy (see 2 Timothy 1:5; 3:15). Explain why the circumcision of Timothy was not a contradiction of the decrees of the Jerusalem Council (see 1 Corinthians 9:19-23).

_____

READ 16:6-12

10. Why did Paul change his plans and go to Macedonia? How do you think his destination affects us today? Describe the city where Paul, Silas, Timothy, and the author, Luke, stayed for several days.

_____

READ 16:13-15

11. Where did Paul find a Jewish prayer meeting? Describe the woman who responded to Paul's message. What indicates a genuine conversion?

_____

READ 16:16-24

12. How did Paul deal with the testimony of a demon? (Read Mark 1:23-25 to see the precedent set by Jesus.) Why were Paul and Silas seized? What reason was given for the seizure to the magistrates? Describe the public humiliation, as well as the cruelty, Paul and Silas experienced.

_____

READ 16:25-34

13. What Christian characteristics were influencial in bringing the jailer to salvation? Who else observed a demonstration of Christian living?

_____

14. Who heard and believed the gospel? What were the evidences of changed lives?

_____

READ 16:35-40

15. How did Paul give proper respect to the gospel?

_____

SUMMARY

How was a cultural problem solved?

Acts 15:2 _____   15:6_____
15:15_____   15:22_____
15:28_____   15:31_____

Who were the members of the Church at Philippi?

Acts 16:14 _____ 16:15_____
16:34_____

APPLICATION

Be challenged by Paul's example in difficulties! He used them as opportunities to praise God and share Jesus Christ.

EVANGELISTIC WORK AT THESSALONICA, BEREA, ATHENS, AND CORINTH

The noble and the pagan, men and women, Jews and Gentiles, responded to the gospel. Those who rejected the message scoffed and angrily attacked the messengers. Devoted friends willingly identified with the gospel and encouraged the missionaries to "be witnesses" (Acts 1:8).

READ 17:1-9

1. How was the gospel presented in Thessalonica? What three groups became believers?

_____

2. Why did the unbelievers instigate opposition? What tactics did they use? What can be observed about the human heart that refuses the gospel?

_____

READ 17:10-14

3. What encouragement did the missionaries receive in Berea? How did the Jews in Berea respond differently to the gospel? Why was the gospel thwarted? Who nurtured the church?

_____

READ 17:15-34

4. Why did Paul feel disturbed while he was in Athens, the center of Greek mythology? Where did he minister, and who were his examiners?

_____

5. Where was Paul invited for a complete hearing? How did his introduction take into account the nature of the audience?

_____

6. What four truths did he present? Describe the varied reactions. What can be observed from Paul's example as to places and methods of presenting the gospel?

_____

_____

READ 18:1-17

7. What trade did Paul practice to support his ministry while in Corinth (see also 1 Corinthians 9:18)? With whom did he live? What fellowship and unity do you think they experienced?

_____

8. What circumstances freed Paul for full-time ministering (see also 2 Corinthians 11:8-9)? What does Paul's example teach about financial difficulties (cf. Philippians 4:12)?

_____

9. From what place did Paul minister when the synagogue was closed to him? What was the three-step response of the Corinthians to the gospel message?

_____

_____

10. How did God encourage and prepare Paul's fearful heart (cf. 1 Corinthians 2:3)? Why was he taken before a Roman provincial governor? How did Gallio's decision to throw the case out of court set a helpful precedent for the missionaries' future work?

_____

_____

READ 18:18-22

11. Who traveled with Paul to Ephesus? (Read Numbers 6 to understand the Nazarite vow. It is not known why Paul took the vow.) How did he conclude his second missionary trip?

_____

READ 18:23-28

12. Who ministered in Ephesus between Paul's two visits? Name at least five characteristics of this great man. How was his instruction limited?

_____

_____

13. What can be learned from the attitude of Aquila and Priscilla toward Apollos and his lack of information about the finished work of Christ? How did Apollos respond when more light was presented?

_____

_____

14. What recommendation did the Ephesians give Apollos?

_____

SUMMARY

As Paul ministered in cities, from what various places did he speak?

Acts 17:1 _____ 17:10_____
17:17_____ 17:19_____
18:4_____ 18:7_____
18:19_____

Name the different kinds of people who believed.

Acts 17:4 _____ 17:12_____
17:34_____ 18:8_____

State the reactions of those who did not believe.

Acts 17:5 _____ 17:13_____
17:18_____ 17:32_____
18:6_____ 18:12_____

APPLICATION

What kind of a friend are you to those who proclaim the gospel? Can you be a Jason, an Aquila or Priscilla, or a Justus? May your strong identification with the gospel enable you to give your home, reputation, and time to aid and encourage those who minister.

THE EPHESIAN CHURCH
ESTABLISHED

In this passage, Luke tells how God used extraordinary methods to confirm His Word in the cities of Ephesus and Troas. He described God's protection and Paul's faithfulness as he and his team continued to "be witnesses" (Acts 1:8).

READ 19:1-7

1. Of whom were the Ephesians uninformed? How was their knowledge of Christ incomplete? (Read in Acts 18:25 of a teacher who was limited in his knowledge.)

2. What was the Ephesians' reaction to Paul's explanation of Christ? (Laying on of hands is not a required pattern to follow, and the work of the Holy Spirit is manifested in various ways, according to 1 Corinthians 12:11. Later, in Ephesians 1:13, Paul stated a principle to the Ephesians concerning the Holy Spirit.)

READ 19:8-10

3. From what places did Paul preach and teach? How often? How far-reaching was his work while in Ephesus?

73

READ 19:11-20

4. What kind of miracles was God performing? How did the Jewish exorcist desire to use the name of Jesus? How did the misuse of Jesus' name, without a committed heart, backfire for the exorcists? How did God use this experience to bring publicity to the gospel?

_____

_____

READ 19:21-22

5. What plans did Paul formulate?

_____

READ 19:23-41

6. How did the gospel affect the economics and religion of the Ephesians? Who agitated the Ephesians? Where did the mob drag Paul's companions?

_____

7. Why wouldn't the crowd listen to Alexander? What indicates the spirit of a mob out of control? Who finally brought some control?

_____

8. What three rational considerations brought the dramatic episode to a conclusion?

_____

_____

READ 20:1-5

9. Follow on a map the journey through Macedonia to the established areas. Who made up the missionary team?

_____

READ 20:6-12

10. For what purpose and when were the Christians at Troas gathered? Describe the conditions conducive for sleep which led to the fall of Eutychus. How was God's power observed?

_____

_____

READ 20:13-21

11. Trace the journey to Ephesus. Whom did Paul address? What did he emphasize in the review of his ministry at Ephesus? What indicates his heart was involved in his work, along with his mind and body?

_____

_____

READ 20:22-27

12. What goals and dangers did Paul share concerning his
    future ministry?

    _____

READ 20:28-35

13. Of what difficulties from within and without did Paul
    warn the elders? What power could the elders know as
    they carried out their responsibilities? How was Paul an
    example in two important attitudes?

    _____

    _____

READ 20:36-38

14. How would this kind of a parting be a source of strength
    for Paul and the Ephesian elders in the difficult days
    ahead?

    _____

SUMMARY

What extraordinary methods did God use to confirm His
Word in the days of the apostles?

Acts 19:6 _____   19:11 _____
19:17 _____   20:12 _____

76

Name the characteristics of Paul's ministry.

Acts 20:19 _____   20:20_____
20:21_____   20:27_____
20:31_____   20:33_____
20:35_____

APPLICATION

You can learn something about yourself and your relationship
to God by your concern with materialism. The unbelieving
Ephesians reacted in an emotional frenzy when their money
was threatened (19:28). Some believing Ephesians burned
their possessions (19:19). Paul said that he coveted no man's
silver or gold or clothing (20:33). Giving God everything will
bring rich blessings of a close relationship.

PAUL IN JERUSALEM

En route to Jerusalem and at the "Holy City" itself, Paul and his Gentile companions were met warmly. But a mob's reaction to a false report brought about Paul's arrest. He used his defense as an opportunity to obey the commission to "be witnesses" (Acts 1:8).

READ 21:1-6

1. At which islands and main port did Paul's party stop? Name the Phoenician city where the party stayed. (Read Acts 11:19 to learn how it was evangelized.)

_____

2. What indicates that a bond was established between Paul's party and the Christians at Tyre even though they had known each other for only a brief time? What concern did the Christians at Tyre have for Paul?

_____

READ 21:7-14

3. What kind of fellowship do you think Philip and Paul's party experienced? (Read Acts 6:5 and Acts 8 to review the work of Philip.) What information did Agabus state in his prophecy? How did friends react to the prophecy? What was Paul's highest consideration (Acts 20:22-24)? Do you think Paul's friends brought warnings or temptations? What were the friends' highest desires?

_____

_____

_____

READ 21:15-26

4. Who greeted the missionaries? What excitement did Paul have to share (see Acts 21:16-17, Romans 15:26)? What reception did they receive on their arrival and after their report?

_____

5. How many Jews were believers? What rumors had caused problems among the Jews? (Read Acts 16:3 for Paul's attitude toward Jewish circumcision.) What indicates James had faith in Paul?

_____

6. What was James's suggestion? Why do you think Paul was willing to execute James's plan? (See 1 Corinthians 9:22.)

_____

READ 21:27-40

7. Why was not the plan completed? How far reaching was the uprising? Who saved Paul's life? How violent was the crowd?

_____

_____

8. How did Paul clear up the misconceptions of the commander?

_____

READ 22:1-5

9. What admirable ability quieted the Jewish listeners? How did Paul describe his past as to place of birth, education, and religious purpose? How would this description bring an identification with this riotous mob?

_____

_____

READ 22:6-16

10. What do you think the purpose of Paul is in telling the details of his conversion (see also Acts 9 for Luke's account)? How would Paul's description of Ananias bring validity to Ananias's words in the mind of the Jews?

_____

READ 22:17-30

11. What part of the speech stirred up the mob again? How did the commander attempt to get some answers?

_____

12. What fact startled the commander? How did Paul aid himself and the commander? Where was he sent?

_____

SUMMARY

How did Paul's friends reveal concern for him?

Acts 21:5 _____ 21:7_____
21:12_____ 21:17_____
21:24_____

How many heard the full story of Christ and conversion while Paul was captive in Jerusalem? (See Acts 22:22.)

Acts 21:30 _____ 21:36_____

APPLICATION

Do you have a Christian philosophy of life? Do you live by it? In this passage Paul illustrated his philosophy, "To testify the gospel of the grace of God" (Acts 20:24), by his actions. May his example be an encouragement to use your circumstances (whether they are fearful, anxious, embarrassing, or pleasurable) to share the riches of Christ.

PAUL'S DEFENSE BEFORE THE SANHEDRIN AND FELIX

Paul gave the same message for his defense, but designed it with an understanding of his listeners. He approached the Sanhedrin with a knowledge of their divided council. He made a logical presentation before Felix, the judge, but talked to Drusilla and Felix alone about their personal needs. He appropriately used each situation to heed the commission to "be witnesses" (Acts 1:8).

READ 23:1-11

1. What personal defense did Paul give to the Sanhedrin the day after his arrest? (Read Luke 22:66-67; Acts 4:5-12; 5:25-32; 6:8-15 for others who stood before the Sanhedrin.) What did the high priest command?

   _____

2. What verbal retort did Paul give? (Read Matthew 23:27 for a similar response by Christ.) What knowledge of the Law did Paul have (see Exodus 22:28)? Why do you think Paul said that he was not aware that Ananias was high priest?

   _____

   _____

82

3. How did Paul create a dissension? Who was concerned for Paul? What protection was given?

_____

4. What experiences in Jerusalem would have seemed defeating? How was Paul comforted at this critical time in his life? (Read 1 Corinthians 3:8 to discover what God blesses.) How has God comforted you when you labored without visible success?

_____

READ 23:12-22

5. Describe the conspiracy against Paul. Name the cooperative people involved in the plot. Whom did God use to hamper the plans?

_____

READ 23:23-35

6. Who made up the procession to Caesarea? What contents in the letter of Claudius Lysias show he protected himself so as to look good in the eyes of his superior? How did Paul's citizenship and birthplace give him protection and an entrance to the Gentiles?

_____

_____

READ 24:1-9

7. Who were Paul's accusers? How did Tertullus use Paul's trial as an opportunity to flatter Felix?

_____

8. What were the Jews' three accusations against Paul? How could Christians today be accused of similar behavior? How did Tertullus distort the truth concerning Lysias?

_____

_____

READ 24:10-21

9. In what manner did Paul approach Felix? What facts did he state as a denial of their first accusation?

_____

10. What statement concerning Paul's belief could the Jews identify with? What evidence was lacking in the third accusation?

_____

READ 24:22-27

11. How did Felix's postponement of a decision calm the Jews? How did it affect Paul?

_____

12. What three elements constituted Paul's challenge to Felix and Drusilla? How did Felix deal with his fear of the truth? What did Felix want for himself and what did he want for the Jews?

_____

_____

SUMMARY

Of what was Paul accused?

Acts 24:5 _____ 24:6_____

What means did he use to defend himself?

Acts 23:6 _____ 24:13_____
24:19_____

What did Paul admit?

Acts 24:14 _____ 24:21_____

APPLICATION

Paul's highest priority was speaking the truth instead of following the natural impulse to preserve his life. The evidences of a successful witness were lacking, but "the Lord stood by his side" and encouraged him for his witness in Jerusalem. May his courage challenge you to be a faithful witness no matter what the response.

PAUL'S DEFENSE BEFORE FESTUS AND AGRIPPA

The new Roman governor of Judea, Festus, wanted good relations with the Jews as proof that he was worthy of the appointment by the emperor, Nero. Festus was willing to give the Jews their way with Paul, but God overruled by means of Paul's Roman citizenship. Paul defended himself twice. He spoke persuasively to King Agrippa and Bernice as he followed the commission to "be witnesses" (Acts 1:8).

READ 25:1-5

1. After Festus took over the governorship, what state visit did he make? What does this indicate about Festus?

_____

2. For what did the Jewish leaders pressure Festus? How long had their hearts desired to kill Paul (see Acts 24:27)? What did Festus propose to assure fairness in the trial?

_____

READ 25:6-12

3. What was lacking again in the Jews' charges against Paul? What three charges did Paul deny? How did Festus reason like his predecessor, Felix (see Acts 24:27)?

_____

_____

4. Why did Paul refuse to go to Jerusalem for a trial (Acts 23:12)? What legal right, as a Roman citizen, did he use?

_____

READ 25:13-27

5. Why did King Agrippa (read of his father in Acts 12:1) and Bernice (older sister of Drusilla, Acts 24:24) come to Caesarea? What kind of an opportunity did this visit give Festus?

_____

6. How did Festus describe the religious issue that caused the Jews to be so revengeful? What desire did King Agrippa state?

_____

7. What showmanship became part of the hearing? Read Acts 12:21-23 and note the likeness between father and son. From Festus's introduction of Paul, what can be learned about the extent of the prisoner's influence?

_____

8. What was the reason for King Agrippa to hear the case?

_____

READ 26:1-11

9. Why did Paul desire to speak before King Agrippa? In what specific ways did Paul and other Jews think alike? Where did their thinking part (Acts 13:32-37)?

_____

_____

10. What was Paul's ambition before his conversion? With what passion did he work?

_____

READ 26:12-18

11. What did Paul see and hear which convinced him of the reality of the resurrected Christ? What stubbornness did Paul express about himself? Give four specific descriptions of what is involved in salvation.

_____

_____

READ 26:19-23

12. Describe the extent of Paul's obedience to Christ.

_____

READ 26:24-32

13. What specific in the defense irritated Festus (Acts 26:23)? How did Paul appeal to King Agrippa? What indicates King Agrippa understood Paul's words?

_____

_____

14. What was Paul's objective during this pompous occasion?

_____

SUMMARY

What was the central issue in the charges against Paul?

Acts 25:19 _____ 26:8_____

What verdict did the judges give Paul?

Acts 25:25 _____ 26:31_____

APPLICATION

Paul's conversion meant a new direction to which he committed himself for a lifetime: "I continue unto this day witnessing to small and great" (Acts 26:22). Is there a commitment to endurance in your Christian life, knowing you have "obtained help of God"? Memorize Acts 26:18 as a reminder of the benefits of salvation and how endurance is possible.

PAUL'S VOYAGE TO ROME

Though Paul's voyage to Rome was hazardous, he maintained spiritual leadership among the prisoners and crew, as well as among the natives of Malta. When the prisoner Paul arrived in Rome, he ministered to his kinsmen, the Roman Jews, and to the Christians. He completed his life writing and teaching of Jesus Christ, and fulfilled his commission to be a witness (Acts 1:8).

READ 27:1-8

1. Who were Paul's fellow passengers on the Adramyttian ship? What was the route of the ship?

   _____

2. What centurion guarded the prisoners? (Compare him with the centurion of Acts 10.) What kindness did he demonstrate?

   _____

3. To what ship were the prisoners transferred? How did the winds affect the voyage to Fair Havens?

   _____

READ 27:9-14

4. What time of year made sailing difficult? What three concerns did Paul have about the continued voyage? From your study in Acts, tell how Paul could give traveling advice from experience. For what reasons did the centurion decide to sail?

_____

_____

READ 27:15-26

5. When the violent northeast wind came down upon the Alexandrian ship, what three safeguards did the crew put into effect? How did they lighten the ship? How desperate was their plight? How did Paul give encouragement?

_____

_____

READ 27:27-44

6. What happened at midnight? How did the sailors attempt to save their own lives? Who was in danger?

_____

7. How was Paul an example of a spiritual leader? What safety was provided for Paul and the other prisoners?

_____

READ 28:1-16

8. What kind of reception did the natives of Melita (Malta) give? What superstitions did the natives attach to the viper?

_____

9. How did Paul demonstrate the power of God? How did the response of the natives to Paul's ministry differ from the responses of others in the book of Acts?

_____

10. How long was the stay at Malta? Who welcomed Paul en route to Rome? What freedom was allowed the prisoner, Paul?

_____

READ 28:17-22

11. In his initial contacts, how did Paul follow the same pattern in Rome as he did elsewhere? Read Romans 1:16, which he had written three years prior to his coming to Rome. What information did the Roman Jews have concerning Paul and Christianity?

_____

READ 28:23-31

12. Where did the Jews gather to hear Paul? How many came? What means did he use to convince them of Christ? For what reason from the Scripture, did some refuse the gospel?

_____

_____

13. What was Paul's ministry in Rome?

_____

SUMMARY

How is the sovereignty of God and human responsibility observed?

Acts 27:24 _____ 27:31 _____

How did Paul maintain spiritual leadership?

Acts 27:22 _____ 27:34 _____
28:9 _____ 28:23 _____
28:31 _____

APPLICATION

Paul fulfilled his task of the commission. "But ye shall receive power after that the Holy Ghost is come upon you; and ye shall be witnesses unto me both in Jerusalem, and in all Judea, and in Samaria, and unto the uttermost part of the earth" (Acts 1:8). May you claim God's power for your life and continue the task to be witnesses!

93